# We Read
## PHONICS™

# Matt and Sid

TREASURE BAY

# Parent's Introduction

Welcome to **We Read Phonics**! This series is designed to help you assist your child in reading. Each book includes a story, as well as some simple word games to play with your child. The games focus on the phonics skills and sight words your child will use in reading the story.

### Here are some recommendations for using this book with your child:

**1 Word Play**

There are word games both before and after the story. Make these games fun and playful. If your child becomes bored or frustrated, play a different game or take a break.

Go...go!

go

go

Excellent!

**Phonics** is a method of sounding out words by blending together letter sounds. However, not all words can be "sounded out." **Sight words** are frequently used words that usually cannot be sounded out.

## ② Read the Story

After some word play, read the story aloud to your child—or read the story together, by reading aloud at the same time or by taking turns. As you and your child read, move your finger under the words.

Next, have your child read the entire story to you while you follow along with your finger under the words. If there is some difficulty with a word, either help your child to sound it out or wait about five seconds and then say the word.

## ③ Discuss and Read Again

After reading the story, talk about it with your child. Ask questions like, "What happened in the story?" and "What was the best part?" It will be helpful for your child to read this story to you several times. Another great way for your child to practice is by reading the book to a younger sibling, a pet, or even a stuffed animal!

This time, let's read the story together!

**LEVEL 1**   **Level 1** focuses on simple words with short "a" and short "i" (as in *cat* and *sit*). Consonants used at this level include b, c, d, f, h, m, n, p, r, s, and t.

# Matt and Sid

A We Read Phonics™ Book
Level 1

_____

Text Copyright © 2010 by Treasure Bay, Inc.
Illustrations Copyright © 2010 by Larry Reinhart

Reading Consultants: Bruce Johnson, M.Ed., and Dorothy Taguchi, Ph.D.

We Read Phonics™ is a trademark of Treasure Bay, Inc.

Published by
Treasure Bay, Inc.
P.O. Box 119
Novato, CA 94948 USA

Printed in Singapore

Library of Congress Catalog Card Number: 2009929508

Hardcover ISBN: 978-1-60115-315-9
Paperback ISBN: 978-1-60115-316-6

Visit us online at:
www.TreasureBayBooks.com

PR 11-09

# Matt and Sid

**By Sindy McKay**

**Illustrated by Larry Reinhart**

# Alphabet Soup

Creating words using certain letters will help your child read this story.

**Materials:** thick paper or cardboard; scissors; pencils, crayons, or markers; small cooking pot, stirring spoon

1. Cut 2 x 2 inch squares from the paper or cardboard and print these letters on the squares: a, i, s, b, c, d, f, g, h, m, n, p, r, and t.

2. One player takes the letter "a." The other player takes the letter "i." Place the other letters into a pretend pot of soup.

3. Players stir the letters. Each player takes a letter from the pot. Stir again. Each player takes another letter. When a player can make a word by putting his letters together, he makes and reads the word out loud.

4. Continue stirring. Each player continues to take additional letters and make words.

Words that can be made with these letters include mat, cab, map, sit, cap, can, bad, fit, mad, sad, tap, and tip.

# Sight Word Game

# Memory

This is a fun way to practice recognizing some sight words used in the story.

1. Write each word listed on the right on two plain 3 x 5 inch cards, so you have two sets of cards. Using one set of cards, ask your child to repeat each word after you. Shuffle both decks of cards together, and place them face down on a flat surface.

2. The first player turns over one card and says the word, then turns over a second card and says the word. If the cards match, the player takes those cards and continues to play. If they don't match, both cards are turned over, and it's the next player's turn.

3. Keep the cards. You can make more cards with other **We Read Phonics** books and combine the cards for even bigger games!

stop

so

that

to

too

now

go

the

has

Matt has a cab.

Sid has a map.

Go fast, Matt!

Matt sits.

Matt adds a cap.

8

Go, Matt, go!

Matt can go fast!

Matt hits a dip.

A map can rip.

That is too bad!

Sid has a fit!

Matt stops the cab.

Sid is so mad!

Sid rips his hat!

Matt is so sad.

A hand taps Sid.

It is Sid's dad!

Now Sid is glad!

Sid tips Matt.

Matt is glad, too!

# Taking a Trip

What else rhymes with cap?

Tap!

Practicing rhyming words helps children learn how words are similar.

1. Explain to your child that these words rhyme because they have the same end sounds: *Matt, bat, cat, chat, flat, hat, pat, rat, sat,* and *that.*

2. Think of a one-syllable simple person, place, or thing from the book.

3. Say: "I am taking a trip. You can join me if you can think of something that rhymes with this person, place, or thing from the book." For example, for the word *Matt,* say: "I am taking a trip. You can join me if you can say a word that rhymes with *Matt.*" If your child has trouble, offer some possible answers or repeat step 1.

4. When your child is successful, repeat step 2 with these words:

   Sid       (possible answers: *bid, did, hid, lid, mid, rid*)

   map      (possible answers: *cap, gap, lap, nap, rap, sap, tap*)

   dip       (possible answers: *flip, hip, lip, nip, rip, sip, tip*)

   fit        (possible answers: *bit, hit, kit, lit, mitt, knit, pit, sit*)

# Phonics Game

## Head Waist Toe

This is a fun way to practice breaking words into parts, which helps children learn to read new words.

Ssss...

iiii...

...d!

1. Stand up facing your child. Make sure you have plenty of room.

2. Choose a simple three-letter word from the story.

3. Each of you touches your head for the first sound, your waist for the middle sound, and your toes for the final sound.

4. For example, for the word *Sid*, say the word, repeat the word, and touch your head when saying the "s" sound, your waist when saying the short "i" sound (as in *fit*), and your toes when saying the "d" sound.

5. Continue with additional words from the story, such as *map*, *has*, *cap*, *dip*, *rip*, *bad*, *fit*, *cab*, *mad*, and *hat*.

If you liked **Matt and Sid,**
here is another **We Read Phonics** book you are sure to enjoy!

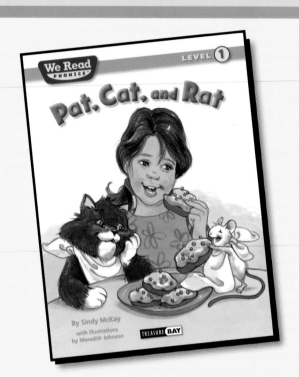

## Pat, Cat, and Rat

This Level 1 book is perfect for the very beginning
reader. In the story, Cat wants to catch Rat and
turn him into a tasty snack, but Pat is determined
to prevent it! The story is simple and easy to read,
and offers lots of humor that is sure to captivate
young readers!